Dear Parent:
Your child's love of reading starts here!

Every child learns to read in a different way and at his or her own speed. You can help your young reader improve and become more confident by encouraging his or her own interests and abilities. You can also guide your child's spiritual development by reading stories with biblical values and Bible stories, like I Can Read! books published by Zonderkidz. From books your child reads with you to the first books he or she reads alone, there are I Can Read! books for every stage of reading:

SHARED READING
Basic language, word repetition, and whimsical illustrations, ideal for sharing with your emergent reader.

BEGINNING READING
Short sentences, familiar words, and simple concepts for children eager to read on their own.

READING WITH HELP
Engaging stories, longer sentences, and language play for developing readers.

READING ALONE
Complex plots, challenging vocabulary, and high-interest topics for the independent reader.

ADVANCED READING
Short paragraphs, chapters, and exciting themes for the perfect bridge to chapter books.

I Can Read! books have introduced children to the joy of reading since 1957. Featuring award-winning authors and illustrators and a fabulous cast of beloved characters, I Can Read! books set the standard for beginning readers.

A lifetime of discovery begins with the magical words **"I Can Read!"**

Visit www.icanread.com for information on enriching your child's reading experience.
Visit www.zonderkidz.com for more Zonderkidz I Can Read! titles.

He [God] gives grace to those
who are not proud.
—*Proverbs 3:34*

ZONDERKIDZ

The Princess Twins and the Tea Party
Copyright © 2011 by Mona Hodgson
Illustrations © 2016 by Julie Olson

Requests for information should be addressed to:
Zonderkidz, 3900 Sparks Dr. SE, Grand Rapids, Michigan 49546

This edition: ISBN 978-0-310-75038-3 (softcover)

This edition: ISBN 978-0-310-75310-0 (hardcover)

Library of Congress Cataloging-in-Publication Data

Hodgson, Mona Gansber, 1954–
    The princess twins and the tea party / by Mona Hodgson.
        p. cm. — (I can read!)
    Summary: When Emma tries to make sure that everything is perfect for the princess twins' tea party, Abby reminds her only God is perfect.
        ISBN 978-0-310-72711-8 (softcover)
    [1. Princesses—Fiction. 2. Twins—Fiction. 3. Sisters—Fiction. 4. Parties—Fiction 5. Christian life—Fiction.] I. Title
    PZ7.H6649Ptp 2012
    [E]—dc22   2010052446

Editor: Mary Hassinger
Art direction & design: Jamie DeBruyn

Printed in China

15 16 17 18 19 20 /DHC/ 7 6 5 4 3 2 1

I Can Read! 1 BEGINNING READING

The Princess Twins
and the Tea Party

Story by Mona Hodgson / Pictures by Julie Olson

Princess Emma dressed up.

Today was the Spring Tea.

Emma wanted everything
to be perfect.

She ran to the castle kitchen.

The cook was making the cakes.

"Did you remember the sugar?"

Emma asked.

The cook stopped stirring.

"Of course I added the sugar,"

he said.

"I just want things to taste right,"

said Emma.

"They will taste good,"

the cook said.

Emma ran to the tea room.

The table looked pretty,

but the napkins didn't look right.

Emma unfolded them.

Then she folded them her way.

Puppy ran into the tea room.

"You don't belong in here,"

said Emma.

"You could ruin the tea party."

She picked up Puppy

and set him outside.

Emma went back to the tea room.

Where were the name cards?

Where was her sister Abby?

Emma ran to find her sister.

She ran right into Abby.

The name cards flew to the floor.

"Now we have to make new cards,"

said Emma.

Abby picked up the cards.

"There's nothing wrong with these,"

she said.

"I want everything to be perfect," said Emma.

"Only God is perfect," Abby said.

Abby set the name cards by the cups.

"Don't worry, Emma.

Just enjoy the party," said Abby.

The castle bell rang.

The princesses ran to the door.

Princess Emma and Princess Abby

took their friends to the tea room.

Everything was perfect.

Then Emma saw Puppy by the table.

She tried to grab Puppy.

Instead, Emma stepped on his tail.

Puppy wiggled. Emma wobbled.

Then Emma bumped the table.

The table tumbled to the floor.

Tea splashed in a puddle.

Puppy slurped tea.

"Welcome to Puppy's perfect party," said Abby.

Emma giggled.

The other girls giggled too.

Then they enjoyed sweet tea

and yummy applesauce cake.